SCHIRMER'S LIBRARY
OF MUSICAL CLASSICS

WOLFGANG AMADEUS MOZART

Concertos

For the Piano

Critically Revised, Fingered, and
the Orchestral Accompaniments
Arranged for a Second Piano by

by FRANZ KULLAK
AND OTHERS

G. SCHIRMER, Inc.

DISTRIBUTED BY
HAL•LEONARD®
CORPORATION
7777 W. BLUEMOUND RD. P.O. BOX 13819 MILWAUKEE, WI 53213

This is Mozart's last piano concerto. It was completed January 5, 1791, and first performed on March 4, with the composer at the piano.

Concerto in B♭ Major
for Piano and Orchestra
[K.595]

Edited by
Isidor Philipp

Wolfgang Amadeus Mozart
1756 - 1791

41546 Cx

41546

Cadenza by W. A. Mozart

41546

41546

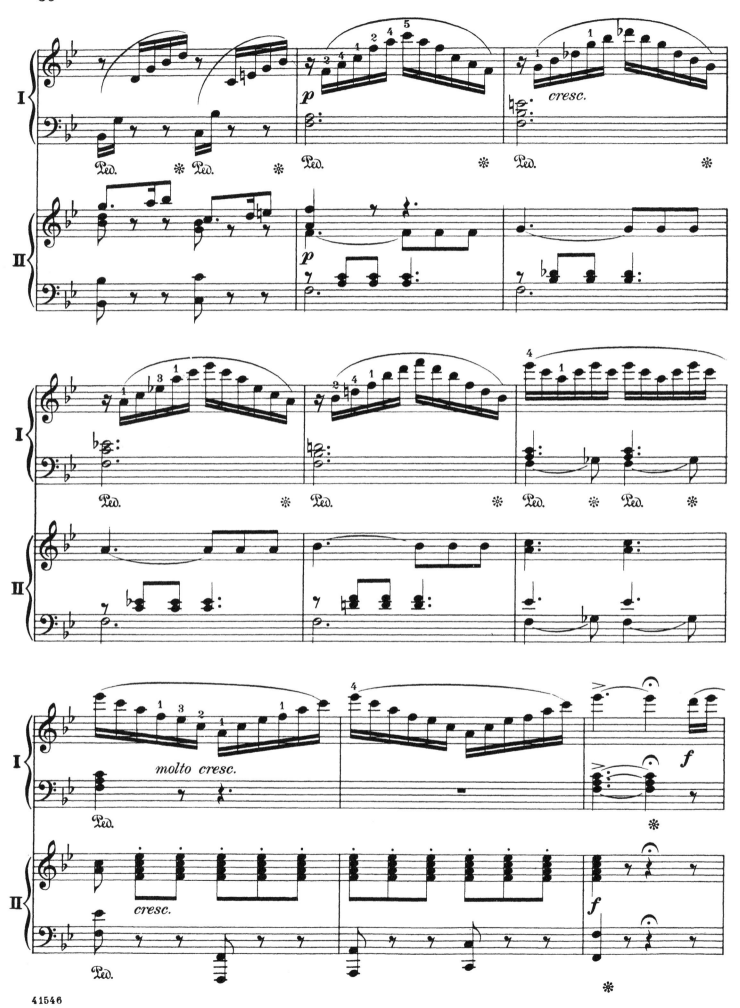

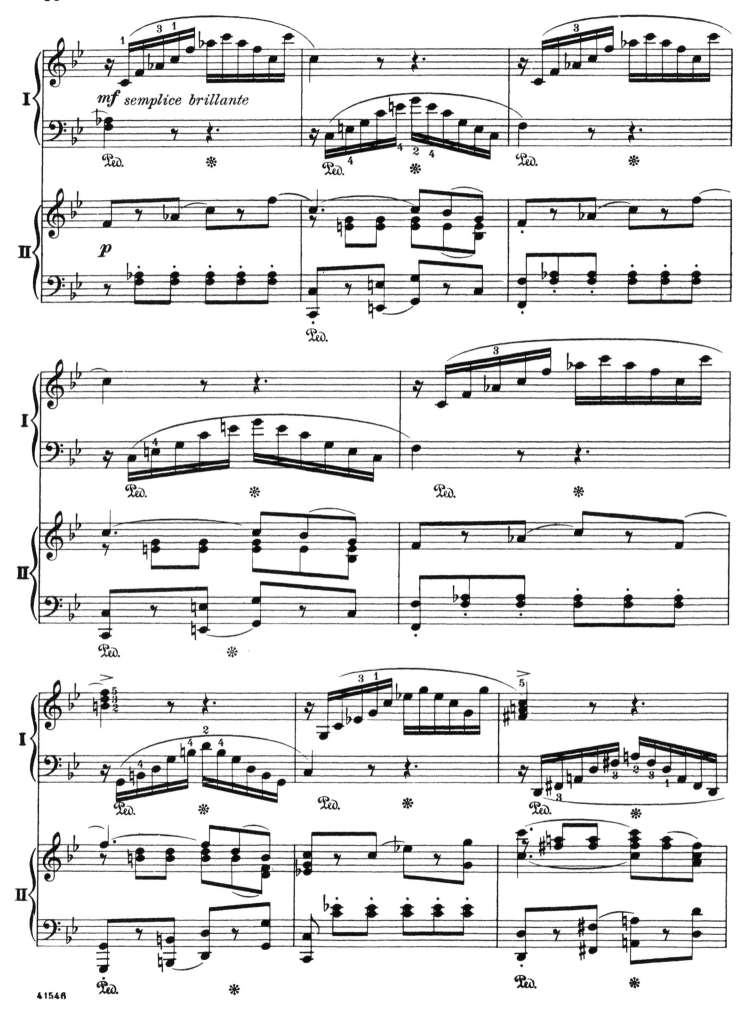

Cadenza by W. A. Mozart